Fact Finders®

Amusement Park Science

SIMPLE MACHINES
at the
AMUSEMENT PARK
by Tammy Enz

CAPSTONE PRESS
a capstone imprint

Fact Finders Books are published by Capstone Press,
1710 Roe Crest Drive,
North Mankato, Minnesota 56003
www.capstonepub.com

Library of Congress Cataloging-in-Publication Data

Names: Enz, Tammy, author.

Title: Simple machines at the amusement park / by Tammy Enz.

Description: North Mankato, Minnesota : Capstone Press, [2020] | Audience: Ages 8-11. | Audience: Grades 4-6.

Identifiers: LCCN 2018060535| ISBN 9781543572827 (hardcover) | ISBN 9781543575262 (pbk.) | ISBN 9781543572865 (ebook pdf)

Subjects: LCSH: Simple machines—Juvenile literature. | Amusement rides—Juvenile literature.

Classification: LCC TJ147 .E588 2020 | DDC 791.06/80284—dc23

LC record available at https://lccn.loc.gov/2018060535

Editorial Credits

Carrie Braulick Sheely, editor; Tracy McCabe, designer; Eric Gohl, media researcher; Kathy McColley, production specialist

Photo Credits

Alamy: Isaac74, 9 (bottom), Q-Images, 9 (top), Richard Green, 17; Capstone: 7; Getty Images: Dorling Kindersley, 15; iStockphoto: Aneese, 29, onfilm, 21, PIMpoon9, 27; Newscom: John Greim Photography, 19; Shutterstock: Colin Dewar, back cover (background), 1 (background), 11, corbac40, 25 (bottom), Dana Ward, 25 (top), footageclips, 5, Gyvafoto, 20, Hintau Aliaksei, 22, Krylovochka, cover (bottom), 1 (bottom), Rudmer Zwerver, 23, Sanga Park, cover (top), 13, Sergey Edentod, 14

Design Elements: Shutterstock

Printed in the United States   4410

TABLE OF CONTENTS

CHAPTER 1

NOT SO SIMPLE

It's time for a fun-filled day. You're about to enter an amusement park! As you step through the gate, you see motion in all directions. Roller coasters zip down hills and through loops. The Ferris wheel goes round and round. As you take in all the sights and sounds, you might not notice the parts that make up these exciting rides. But if you look closely, you'll discover that much of the stomach-dropping fun at an amusement park relies on simple machines.

Not sure you can spot them? Settle in and keep your eyes peeled. By the time the day is over, you'll be spotting simple machines wherever you go!

What Are Simple Machines?

Amusement parks are all about fun, right? Of course! But for us to have fun, machines have to do work. All simple machines make work easier for us.

A simple machine can work in different ways. It can change the direction or the magnitude of a force. A force is a push or a pull. The magnitude describes the size of the force. A simple machine can create big effects from small twists, turns, or pulls. By changing the direction of a force, a simple machine can get something turning, twisting, or spinning without much effort.

force—a push or pull

magnitude—the size of something

The Ferris wheel is one of the tallest rides at an amusement park. It's also a simple machine!

What's the secret that makes simple machines do what they do? Simple machines use mechanical advantage. This means they reduce work. Work is what's done when a force moves something. Mechanical advantage allows you to use a little force to get a big payoff.

There are six simple machines. These are pulleys, levers, wedges, inclined planes, wheels and axles, and screws. Each machine does a lot of work. And when simple machines work together, they can create nonstop fun at an amusement park.

---

axle—a bar in the center of a wheel around which a wheel turns

inclined plane—a sloped surface

lever—a bar that turns on a resting point and is used to lift items

mechanical advantage—ability of a machine to reduce work

pulley—a grooved wheel turned by a rope, belt, or chain

screw—an inclined plane wrapped around a post that usually holds objects together

wedge—a device that moves to split things apart

SIMPLE MACHINES

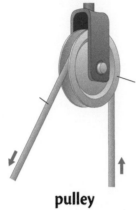

pulley

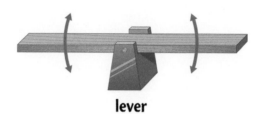

lever

inclined plane

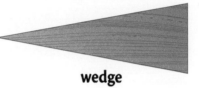

wedge

wheel and axle

screw

CHAPTER 2

PULL UP

Raise the Flags

Before you even walk through the front gate of an amusement park, you've already seen the work of a simple machine. Where? Look up. Do you see the row of flags waving over the park? Have you ever wondered how those flags got there? Do you suppose a worker went all the way up there to hang the flags? More likely a pulley lifted them into place.

Pulley systems are attached to flagpoles. A pulley uses a grooved wheel looped with a cable to change the direction of a force. How does it do this? There is a wheel at the top of the flagpole. A cable wraps around it. As the worker pulls down on the cable, the flag goes up.

Six flags wave over the Six Flags Over Texas amusement park. They are the flags of the different countries that have governed what is now Texas.

HUMAN-POWERED PARK

You can be a machine too! Take a trip to northern Italy. There you'll find the Ai Pioppi amusement park. Except for just one ride, it is totally powered by humans and simple machines such as pulleys and levers. The park is filled with roller coasters, carousels, and other rides. But you won't find motors or electricity. People power all the rides with their legs and arms. Thankfully, the force of **gravity** acts on some rides to give visitors a rest and some hard-earned fun!

gravity—a force that pulls objects with mass together; gravity pulls objects down toward the center of Earth

Pulleys on Rides

Pulleys help with more than just raising flags. *Clack. Clack. Clack.* You know that noise! It's a roller coaster slowly climbing the first big hill. But guess what's pulling it up to that death-defying height? It's a pulley. The pulley that lifts a roller coaster is a chain wrapped around a gear. A motor turns the gear. The teeth in the gear grab the chain and pull it. This action lifts the ride in the same way a flag is raised.

The Zipper is one of the wildest rides at the amusement park. Cars zip along on a spinning boom. A motor provides power to spin the wheels on each end of the boom. The cable pulls the cars around the wheels. What is the point of this pulley action? It causes one of the scariest parts of the ride—the flipping of the cars as they speed around the boom ends.

boom—a long beam connected to a support

gear—a toothed wheel that fits into another toothed wheel; gears can change the direction of a force or can transfer power

A cable brings the cars around the boom of the Zipper ride.

BLOCK AND TACKLE

If one pulley is good, more than one is better. When two or more pulleys are connected by a single cable, the mechanical advantage is even greater. The mechanical device created by using more than one pulley is called a block and tackle. Each additional pulley reduces the force needed to lift something. Two pulleys require half the force. Four pulleys require one-quarter of the force.

CHAPTER 3

WHEEL AROUND

Wheel and Axle

As you lurch to the top of the Ferris wheel, you can gaze out for miles. But if you look down, you can see another simple machine at work. You're riding on it! The Ferris wheel is a simple machine called a wheel and axle.

In a wheel and axle, a large circle, or wheel, is attached to a rod called an axle. The spin of the axle moves the large wheel. A little spin on the axle causes big movement of the wheel. The wheel and axle rotate at the same rate. But the larger wheel turns over a greater distance than the axle. On a Ferris wheel, a motor usually provides power to spin the axle.

Wheels and axles are everywhere at an amusement park. The entertainer on a unicycle uses physical force on the axle to get the wheel turning. The brightly lit carousel spins on an axle.

The Ferris wheel turns around a huge axle at its middle.

For a double-axle thrill check out the Scrambler. On this ride you'll spin in cars attached to a small wheel and axle. At the same time a larger wheel and axle in the center of the ride spins.

FACT

Want the fastest ride on the carousel? Pick a horse on the outside of the ride. The outside horses travel the fastest. Why? All the horses must travel around the circle in the same amount of time, but those on the outside have farther to go. They have to travel faster.

More Than One Way to Work

Wheels help reduce work in other ways too. Imagine trying to pull or push a bulky concession stand without wheels across the amusement park. Its bottom would scrape across the ground. This would create a force called friction. Friction is a resisting force caused when two objects rub together. It would make your stand hard to move.

A concession stand on wheels moves easily around the park. Only the wheels touch the ground. Wheels reduce friction. They make it much easier to move things. The bigger the wheels, the easier the stand will be to push. Larger wheels give you more pushing force and overcome friction better than small wheels.

Wheels and axles on carts and concession stands help workers move them around a park easily.

Now head over to the restrooms. Grab the doorknob and turn it. There's no need to go any farther! You just used a wheel and axle. As you spun the knob, it created a force in the axle.

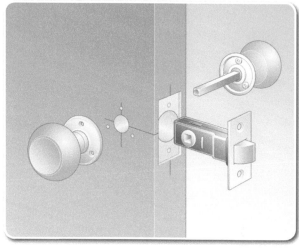

Inside a doorknob, an axle turns to release a latch.

This force opened the latch to open the door. In this case you supplied a force to the outside of the wheel, and it turned the axle. The force on the axle was much larger than you could have supplied by turning the axle without a knob. The bigger the doorknob, the greater the force you can supply to the axle when turning it.

friction—a force created when two objects rub together

CHAPTER 4

LIFT AND WEDGE

Up the Inclined Plane

Scramble up the ramp as you rush to find a seat on the Tilt-a-Whirl. You probably never noticed the simple machine right at your feet! The ramp is called an inclined plane.

An inclined plane is a sloped surface. It has no moving parts. But that doesn't mean it can't help lessen the effort required to do something. It takes less force to move something up an inclined plane than lifting it straight up. With little effort you can race right up a ramp to get to the top of a platform. Imagine the work it would take to try to climb or jump up there without a ramp. The longer an inclined plane is, the less effort it takes to move up it. But of course you'll have to travel farther to move higher!

You'll find inclined planes all over the park. Check out the big slides or the hills on the roller coaster track. Toss a ball up the inclined plane at the Skee-Ball game. The inclined plane allows you to gently toss the ball up and position it to hit your target. Workers use ramps to load or unload goods from trucks. The staircases you travel up are inclined planes too. They move you up and down with little effort.

A ball zips up the inclined plane of a Skee-Ball game.

Down the Inclined Plane

Imagine dropping straight down from the top of the log flume ride. The landing would likely be really hard! Instead the log travels along an inclined plane. It makes the landing gentler.

An inclined plane works against the force of gravity to help you safely move down from a high place. As you go down a slide, gravity tries to pull you straight down. But friction slows your movement down the inclined plane. Even the force from the inclined plane pushing back on you reduces gravity's effect. You can move safely down the slide.

MORE INCLINED PLANES

An inclined plane doesn't have to be straight like a ramp. Have you ever driven up a mountain? The road twists around the mountain to move you very high with ease. The road is like a ramp, but it twists its way around instead of running straight up.

A log flume ride uses an inclined plane to help riders travel safely downward.

FACT

The longest slide in the world is in London, England. It stands 256 feet (78 meters) tall and is 584 feet (178 meters) long. Part of it is shaped like a corkscrew.

Wedges

Have you ever tried to ride side by side with a friend on the bumper cars? What happens if somebody tries pushing his or her car between yours? If the incoming car is able to create a small amount of separation, he or she can likely wedge in and push your cars even farther apart. This separation is caused by wedge action.

A wedge is a simple machine that causes separation by changing the direction of a force. Wedges are thicker on one end and tapered to a point on the other. An example is the ax the scary guy is holding at the haunted house. Outside the amusement park, an ax works to separate a chunk of wood into pieces. It changes a downward force into sideways pushing forces. That's its mechanical advantage.

When one bumper car pushes between two other cars, the middle car is acting like a wedge. Most wedges push things apart.

Ready for a cool drink or a tasty snack? The knife used to cut lemon slices for your lemonade is another wedge. Are you ready to grab a slice of pizza? A concession stand worker might have used a wedge called a pizza rocker to cut it. You can even use your thumb as a wedge to pry apart a peanut shell to get to the peanut inside.

CHAPTER 5

FLIP AND TWIST

Screws

Don't forget to head over to the entertainment tent to watch a show. But before you step into the tent, check out the anchors that hold it to the ground. Likely these anchors are screws, another simple machine.

A screw is a simple machine with spiraled threads. Usually the threads wrap around a solid core. But some screws, such as corkscrews, are open spirals.

When a screw is twisted, its threads easily force their way into a solid object. A screw changes a twist into forward movement. Screws allow a small twist to become a big force. For the workers setting up a tent, twisting the anchors into the ground is much easier than pounding them in.

You'll see screws all over the amusement park. Many metal parts of rides are held together with screws. Screws hold the parts of benches together. Screws also spiral into wood or metal to hang signs.

thread—the spiral part of a screw

Some tent cables are held by screws that twist into the ground.

Levers

You're up! Then you're down! And now you're hanging over the edge of a building more than 850 feet (259 meters) in the air! You are on the X-Scream on top of the Stratosphere in Las Vegas, Nevada. This hair-raising ride acts like a lever to change the ride's directions. A lever is a simple machine that uses a beam and a fulcrum. A beam is a long, straight piece. A fulcrum causes a beam to turn, or pivot. A lever reduces the amount of effort needed to lift a load.

Have you ever been on a seesaw? Then you've seen a lever in action. You and a friend sit on the ends of the beam. The center of the beam is connected to the fulcrum. As you push up, your friend is forced down.

beam—a long, heavy piece of wood, metal, or other material used for support

fulcrum—the place where a lever pivots

The X-Scream hangs riders off the top of the Stratosphere in Las Vegas, Nevada.

THREE CLASSES OF LEVERS

There are three classes of levers. Each one has the load and fulcrum in a different location. In a class 1 lever the fulcrum is placed between the effort and load. In a class 2 lever the load is between the effort and the fulcrum. In a class 3 lever the effort is between the load and the fulcrum.

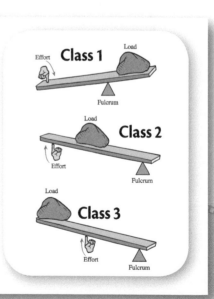

Not all levers look the same. The fulcrum is not always in the middle of the beam. Shovel some slushy into your mouth. As you dig into this frozen treat, you are using a lever. When you take a scoop, your hand is the fulcrum. When you push down, the spoon lifts the treat out of the cone. The force you apply is magnified by the pivoting spoon.

Levers aren't just used as part of amusement park rides. You see ride operators pushing or pulling levers to start and stop rides. Levers are often used for light switches. When you flip the end of a switch, the fulcrum at its base turns the power on or off. In some rides you get to control how high you go. You use a lever to control your height.

A spoon is a type of lever.

FACT
Many levers are used as tools. A crowbar is a lever that can easily pull out a nail.

CHAPTER 6

ADD THEM UP

There's no doubt that simple machines amp up the fun at an amusement park. But simple machines don't always do the work alone. More than one simple machine can work together. When simple machines work together, they make a complex machine. Many rides and attractions use wheels and axles, pulleys, and levers together. Hop on a roller coaster. It uses pulleys and inclined planes for heart-pounding fun.

Wherever you go at an amusement park, you'll see machines. Whether simple or complex, machines work for you. Now you know where to find them at an amusement park. Where else can you find these machines working for you?

A pulley system pulls cars up the ThunderBolt roller coaster in Brooklyn, New York. Riders experience a vertical drop.

complex machine—a machine that uses two or more simple machines

GLOSSARY

axle (AK-suhl)—a bar in the center of a wheel around which a wheel turns

beam (BEEM)—a long, heavy piece of wood, metal, or other material used for support

boom (BOOM)—a long beam connected to a support

complex machine (KAHM-pleks muh-SHEEN)—a machine that uses two or more simple machines

force (FORS)—a push or pull

friction (FRIK-shuhn)—a force created when two objects rub together

fulcrum (FUL-kruhm)—the place where a lever pivots

gear (GEER)—a toothed wheel that fits into another toothed wheel; gears can change the direction of a force or can transfer power

gravity (GRAV-uh-tee)—a force that pulls objects with mass together; gravity pulls objects down toward the center of Earth

inclined plane (in-KLINDE PLANE)—a sloped surface

lever (LEV-ur)—a bar that turns on a resting point and is used to lift items

magnitude (MAG-nuh-tood)—the size of something

mechanical advantage (muh-KAN-uh-kuhl uhd-VAN-tij)—ability of a machine to reduce work

pulley (PUL-ee)—a grooved wheel turned by a rope, belt, or chain

screw (SKROO)—an inclined plane wrapped around a post that usually holds objects together

thread (THRED)—the spiral part of a screw

wedge (WEDGE)—a device that moves to split things apart

READ MORE

Doudna, Kelly. *The Kids' Book of Simple Machines: Cool Projects and Activities That Make Science Fun!* Minneapolis: Mighty Media Kids, 2015.

Roby, Cynthia. *Discovering STEM at the Amusement Park.* STEM in the Real World. New York: PowerKids Press, 2016.

Troupe, Thomas Kingsley. *Keep It Simple, Rapunzel!: The Fairy-Tale Physics of Simple Machines.* STEM-Twisted Fairy Tales. North Mankato, MN: Picture Window Books, 2018.

CRITICAL THINKING QUESTIONS

1. Tilt-a-Whirl cars spin on a wavy platform as they rotate in a circle. What simple machines are at work on this ride?

2. Name two simple machines that could help you get to the top of a skyscraper.

3. What do you think would happen if you moved the fulcrum of a lever? Use online or other sources to support your answer.

INTERNET SITES

All About Simple Machines: Types and Functions
https://easyscienceforkids.com/all-about-simple-machines/

Simple Machines: Facts
http://idahoptv.org/sciencetrek/topics/simple_machines/facts.cfm

Simple Machines
https://www.pbs.org/video/science-trek-simple-machines/

INDEX